ALSO FROM UK DF

CW00855032

LEARNING TO DRIVE:

Teaching a Learner Driver –
A Guide for Amateur Instructors
Learning to Drive –
The Learner Driver's Manual
Teach Yourself Traffic Signs
& Road Markings
The Learner Driver's Logbook –
Lesson Plan & Progress Record
The Driving Test & How to Pass –
An Examiner's Guide to the 'L' Test

250 THEORY TEST QUESTIONS:

Cars - Motorcycles - LGV - PCV - ADI

HIGHWAY CODE & THEORY TEST QUESTIONS:

Cars - Motorcycles - LGV - PCV - ADI

The Highway Code
How to Drive on a Motorway
Driving at Night & in Bad Weather

All available from www.ukdrivingskills.co.uk

Driving at Night & in Bad Weather
Including Highway Code Rules

UK Driving Skills
Glovebox Guides

Don L. Gates

www.ukdrivingskills.co.uk

Revised: 21/08/23

GLOVEBOX GUIDES

Driving at Night & in Bad Weather

1st edition copyright © 2018 Don L. Gates
2nd edition copyright © 2020 Don L. Gates
3rd edition copyright © 2021 Don L. Gates
4th edition copyright © 2022 Don L. Gates

Contents

Introduction

Driving at night for the first time can be a strange experience, more so if like me, you learned to drive during the summer when days were long, and your first night journey is made without anyone there to guide you.

Even after gaining experience, many drivers still go about in darkness as if the sun were shining; showing no regard for the extra demands that driving at night makes on us.

During the spring and summer months the weather is at worst wet and windy, but driving in winter can present a whole new set of problems. An inexperienced driver's first encounter with the perils of winter motoring can be a daunting time, for those unprepared and lacking in the basic knowledge of how to cope with such conditions the results can be deadly.

So here are a few rules and tips for new and seasoned motorists alike, to try and make night time and winter driving a more pleasant...and safer experience!

Part One – Driving at Night

Driving at Night

Before Driving at Night

Maintaining all lights in good working order is a basic legal requirement, but when was the last time you checked yours? How often do we see cars on the roads with only one brake light working, or even one headlight?

All lights should be checked on a regular basis, and it really is easy. All you have to do is turn the ignition on, and then check each light in turn by operating the switch or brake pedal and looking for reflections in adjacent vehicles or other reflective surfaces around you. A quick check like this is fine, but if you're not sure whether a light is working, get out of the car and have a look, or get someone to help you with the check.

If you discover a light isn't working, fix the problem before you set off. A well prepared driver should always carry a spare set of bulbs. Most are simple to change, though if you encounter problems, trained people at motoring accessory shops will usually fit it for you for a small fee. They also carry bulb packs specifically for each make and model of car; make sure you have one, and if you have to use a spare, don't forget to replace it!

It's also advisable to carry a torch at night, especially if you intend to drive where there's no street lighting.

Another sensible precaution before setting out at night is to make sure that your windows are clean. This is not only common sense, but required by law. Dirty windows can directly restrict vision in the best of conditions, but when the headlights from other vehicles are scattered across the glass by the particles of dirt, it can produce a dazzling and impenetrable glare. Badly scratched or cracked windscreens can also have this effect.

Many people make the mistake of wiping a steamed up windscreen with the back of their hand; the natural oils in your skin will actually leave smears across the glass and this again will produce glare when hit by headlights and can be difficult to remove. Always keep a proper glass cloth or wash leather in your car and use this instead.

You shouldn't use any kind of tinted glasses at night, including so called 'night driving glasses'. These may reduce the glare from headlights, but also reduce the level of most other forms of light reaching your eyes; you may as well wear sunglasses!

Visibility

There is one small advantage of driving at night, a glint of headlights around a corner may warn you of the approach of a vehicle which you may have been unaware of during the day. But if there is *no* light showing, do we assume that nothing is there and take the corner at speed? What if the driver hidden around the corner has just set off and forgotten to turn on their lights?

Making allowances for the lack of visibility at night should start the moment you go out to your car. If you have just left a brightly lit area, your eyes can take a while to adjust. If you have just come out of your garage where a light was on, don't come thundering down the driveway the moment you get in the driving seat; that shadow under the overhanging tree at end of the drive could be a pedestrian.

Take time to get used to the poor light, and when you first set off keep your speed down until your eyes have had time to adjust.

Keeping Vision Clear

Your windows may be nice and clean, but the moment you get into a cold car they can start misting over. Turn your demisters on, and if necessary, wait a while until you have some warm air coming through so that the windows stay clear. Don't forget the rear screen heater if required and open windows if you need to.

Don't drive off until you can see properly all around, even a small patch of condensation at eye level can dangerously get in the way of your view.

Judgement

Judgement of situations needs more careful consideration at night. It's much more difficult to judge speed and distance so be extra careful when emerging from junctions, particularly onto high speed roads.

You must resist the temptation to rely on lights to tell you where everything is, smaller vehicles such as cycles or motorcycles can be cast into shadow by many bright lights around them. You may not know they are there unless you actually make the effort to look for them. Avoid the tendency to react only to what you can see in the lit areas, try to take in the whole picture and always look for movement in the shadows.

You must also bear in mind that as mentioned earlier, people sometimes forget to switch lights on. Unfortunately, there is always a risk of encountering unlit cycles; there are far too many irresponsible riders who show a complete disregard for their own safety by failing to carry lights. This can be even more dangerous if you're emerging from a driveway where a suicidal rider speeds along the footpath as you emerge.

Meeting traffic

Another thing to be aware of on dark narrow roads, is that when you see what you think is a motorcycle coming towards you, just make certain that it isn't actually a car with only one headlight before you try to squeeze through that gap!

Pedestrians

Pedestrians need special consideration at night, more so in areas which are poorly lit; they may step out of the shadows without warning. Be extra vigilant in narrow streets and residential areas where there are lots of parked cars, and keep your speed down. Your speed is particularly important when approaching hazards such as zebra crossings at night, they're not all as brightly lit as they need to be, so ensure that you reduce speed and be ready to stop.

Wherever you are at night, ensure you drive at a speed which enables you to stop comfortably within the distance that you can see to be clear. What is said for pedestrians is certainly true for animals too. Particularly if you're driving along country roads there is always the danger of animals running from the shadows, bear this in mind when deciding what speed to drive at.

Use of Lights

The use of dipped headlights is compulsory on all unlit roads at night. On roads where the street lighting is on, a minimum of sidelights should be used but dipped headlights are better. Don't make the mistake of relying on 'daytime running lights' if your car has them; they're actually quite bright and can dazzle other road users at night.

Don't wait for others to lead the way when it comes to lighting up your vehicle, once light begins to fade then switch on to make sure that others can clearly see you. Remember, the headlights are not just there to help you see, but to help others to see *you*!

You should also use dipped headlights on fast dual-carriageways and motorways, even when they're brightly lit.

Headlights should be switched onto main beam when driving on unlit roads, or to briefly illuminate dark areas on any road, providing you won't dazzle other road users. This is normally done by pushing the indicator or headlight lever forwards. Pull it back to turn them off.

When driving on main beam, keep a lookout for oncoming traffic, and vehicles which you may be gaining on; be ready to dip your lights to avoid dazzling anyone. Make sure you have a good look well ahead before you dip to ensure you're aware of what lies ahead.

When your main beam is turned on, the green light on your dashboard (below left) will be replaced by a blue one (below right).

Dipped beam

Main beam

If you're about to be overtaken while driving on main beam, leave the beam on long enough to help the other driver get a good view of the road ahead, but be ready to dip as soon as they start passing you. If you're the one doing the overtaking, make sure you don't turn your main beam back on *too* early and dazzle the driver you're passing.

One thing drivers tend to forget when using main beam, is that the lights will dazzle *anyone* in their path; including pedestrians, cyclists and anyone else who you may encounter. Show them the same courtesy you would to other drivers and dip until you're past them.

The Headlight Flasher

The headlight flasher is without doubt the most misused control on the car. It's designed to be used as a warning device, just like sounding the horn. It comes into its most useful period at night during the hours of II.30 pm and 7 am when it would be against the law to sound the horn in a built up area.

Unfortunately, most people misinterpret a flash of lights as a signal to go ahead; and sometimes with disastrous consequences. Because of this, you need to be very careful about when and how you flash your lights. It can be useful though in certain situations, such as on the approach to blind corners or narrow places in the road when you're not sure whether anything could be coming the other way. A quick flash of your lights will warn other people that you're approaching. In all other situations, think twice before you flash your lights to warn someone at night.

Avoiding Dazzle

When drivers are dazzled, they can be temporarily blinded for several seconds, easily long enough for an accident to occur. Dazzle from main beam is perhaps the greatest danger. If you do encounter an oncoming driver who neglects to dip, a very brief flash of your lights may serve to remind them. Don't make the mistake of 'retaliating' with your own main beam if they fail to respond.

When oncoming lights do hurt your eyes, looking briefly to the left-hand verge while they pass can help, and if you're being dazzled, always be ready to slow down until you regain normal vision, or stop if necessary and it's safe to do so.

Following Distance

There are things you can do at night to avoid causing unnecessary dazzle to other drivers. One of these is to follow at a respectable distance. Even on dipped beam, your headlights can cause all kinds of problems for the driver in front by being reflected in their mirrors. You should keep far enough back whenever possible, so that your lights fall short of the car ahead.

If you're being followed too closely yourself, you can ease the problem if you have a dipping mirror. A lever on the bottom of the mirror frame will tilt it so that the dazzle is removed. You will still be able to see something of what is behind but the view will more of a 'dark image.' Your mirror should be reset as soon as possible. Some cars now have mirrors which dip automatically when light sensors are triggered.

If you don't have a dipping rear view mirror, all you can do is slow down, and if the situation is bad and you are being blinded, move the mirror aside slightly and look for a safe opportunity to pull over to let the other driver pass.

Lights When Stationary

If you're pulling up to park for any reason, don't leave your headlights on for longer than necessary. The fixed glare of bright lights can be dazzling, especially in a poorly lit area, so turn down to sidelights or 'parking lights'. This is particularly important if you pull up on the right-hand side of the road, as the light beam is angled to the left and will be glaring straight into the eyes of oncoming drivers.

You could also briefly turn down your headlights as a courtesy when you stop to wait for an oncoming vehicle where the road narrows. This would be especially helpful in a dark side street or unlit road where the dazzling effect of lights is more pronounced. Turn back to dipped beam once they've come through.

The dazzling effect of lights on stationary cars can be at its worst in traffic queues at lights and junctions. One of the most infuriating things I find is the driver just in front of you who insists on keeping their foot on the brake pedal all the time. Brake lights are very bright, and by the time they move away you have red spots floating in front of your eyes. So take your foot off the pedal and use your parking brake while you're waiting and save your brake light bulbs!

You can also cut down on the amount of unnecessary light by thoughtful use of indicators. If you're waiting to turn right for example, and the cars at front and rear of the queue are indicating this same intention; do all the ones in between really need to be signalling as well? If all the drivers in between were to indicate just before moving off, their intentions would still be clear but without the prolonged flashing of bright lights.

Parking

In addition to any parking requirements which may be in force by day, some extra rules have to be observed at night.

You MUST NOT leave your car parked on the right-hand side of the road (except in a one-way street). Parking on the left means that your rear reflectors will be highlighted by the approach of other driver's lights.

All vehicles MUST display parking lights when on a road or a lay-by with a speed limit of 40 mph or higher.

Large vehicles generally must have lights on all the time when parked on the road at night. Those below 2500kg laden weight may be parked without lights on a road with a speed limit of 30 mph or less providing that they are:

- at least 10 metres away from any junction, close to the kerb and facing in the direction of the traffic flow
- or in a recognised parking place or lay-by.

One final piece of advice when parking at night, always show due consideration for the neighbours by avoiding unnecessary noise and slamming of doors!

Part Two – Bad Weather

Preparations

When winter arrives, extra demands are placed on both the driver and the vehicle. It's vital that you prepare for the onset of winter by taking a few simple steps and ensuring that any equipment which you need to deal with frost and snow is on hand before the need to use them arises.

Anti-Freeze

One of the first priorities is to check your anti-freeze. Some people think that this is something which only needs to be added in winter, but anti-freeze is in fact simply a part of the coolant that circulates in the engine all year round.

You should ensure that it's kept topped up, but if you haven't had the car serviced for a while, you may also need to check that the fluid is still doing its job. Over time, it can lose its efficiency. You can check this using equipment obtainable from motoring accessory shops. If your anti-freeze isn't up to strength, or you're in doubt about its effectiveness, then you may need to flush the cooling system through and replace with fresh fluid. Carrying out this kind of work may not be for everyone, so a simpler solution would be to take your car to a garage and ask them to carry out a winter driving check for you.

Washer Bottles

You can certainly expect to be using your windscreen washers more frequently during bad weather; and because of this it's important to ensure that the reservoir is kept topped up. It's always worthwhile carrying a plastic bottle in the boot filled with water and a suitable additive ready for this purpose, though most of the time now a ready mixed solution can be bought.

An additive is essential for two reasons, firstly it increases the cleaning power and will remove dirt from the screen that water alone wouldn't touch, and much more importantly, it will prevent the water from freezing in cold weather. It's illegal to drive your vehicle if the washers are frozen.

You should only use an additive recommended specifically for this job, the anti-freeze which goes into the cooling system is of a different nature and must not be put into the windscreen washer reservoir.

Tyres

When was the last time you checked the tread on your tyres?
The minimum depth of tread required by law is 1.6 mm across
the central three quarters of the tyre, with tread at least visible
on the rest. If you're driving around on firm, dry roads all the
time this may be sufficient to keep you on the side of safety, but
is it enough to keep a grip on snow and ice?

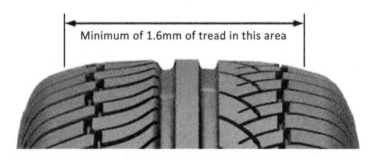

Minimum of 1.6mm of tread in this area

Make sure you have plenty of tread on all your tyres, including
the spare. You can check the tread a number of ways; though
using a small tool called a tread depth gauge is the best. As a
rough guide you can insert a 20p piece into the grooves of the
tread and as long as the border around the edge of the coin is not
visible then you should be okay.

There are also 'tread wear indictors' around the tyres. You'll find
small ridges at regular intervals within the grooves all around
the circumference, as shown within the oval marked on the
following diagram. If these become level with the overall surface
of the tyre then it's time to change them.

You also need to check that there are no cuts or bulges in the walls of the tyres, and that they're inflated to the correct pressure. Worn or defective tyres can affect vehicle control badly enough on a good road surface, in winter your life could depend on them so don't hesitate in replacing any or all of your tyres if need be.

Screen Covers & De-icer

If you have to park your car out in the open, overnight frost can be a real problem. Unless you're lucky enough to have a car with a windscreen heater, you should avoid being caught out by having a supply of de-icer in the vehicle; this is widely available in spray cans from all manner of shops. You should also consider keeping spare de-icer in the house, as in particularly cold weather it's possible that your locks may freeze and you won't be able to get the car door open!

A scraper to assist in the rapid removal of snow and ice is also well worth a small investment.

Plastic covers may be used to prevent the glass from frosting over, these range in size from front screen protectors to sheets that envelop the whole of the vehicle. Using these can save time on frosty mornings, and although they may initially be more expensive than cans of de-icer, the cost will even itself out in the long run because they can obviously be used many times.

Sunglasses

The sun is perhaps the most underestimated danger of winter driving. It hangs lower in the sky during these months and has a much more dazzling effect than the higher sun of warmer seasons. Its effect is at its greatest after rain or when there's ice or snow on the ground which reflects its blinding rays from the road surface directly into the driver's eyes.

To combat this, a good pair of sunglasses is a vital aid to safe observation. If you have glasses with lenses which darken in sunlight, do bear in mind that these may not work behind a windscreen because of the ultra-violet rays being filtered out by the glass.

Windscreen visors will also help shield your eyes from the sun, and not everyone realises that these can usually be unclipped at one side so you can swivel them to offer protection through the side window. If you need to use these, remember to put the visor back when you don't need it otherwise it may needlessly block part of your view.

Whenever your vision is restricted by bright sunlight, you must be prepared to reduce speed and exercise extra caution. When emerging from junctions you must be particularly vigilant and

18

spare a moment or two more with observations to be certain that nothing is missed, especially those harder to spot cyclists near to the kerb.

In bright sunlight, it's essential that all windows are kept clean and clear. When the sun falls on glass that is streaked with dirt or condensation it can be almost impossible to see through.

Snow & Ice

The prospect of driving on snow and ice is enough to send a chill down the spine of even the most seasoned motorist. When conditions are extremely bad, it's wise to ask yourself if the journey you're about to make is really necessary. If you really must travel then do so with the utmost care.

One of the first things to consider is the time factor; if you have an appointment to keep or you're on your way to work then you must give yourself more time by setting off earlier than you normally would. If you make the mistake of trying to drive at normal speeds then you probably wouldn't arrive at all... at least not with your vehicle intact!

Apart from needing more time for the journey itself, you'll also need extra time to prepare the car. If it's covered in ice or snow this must be cleared before you can even attempt setting off. Ice should be scraped from all windows, the windscreen in particular will benefit from a spraying of de-icer as this will prevent frost from re-forming on the glass again as you begin to drive away, this can otherwise happen in seconds on a very cold morning.

If the vehicle is covered in snow, then again this must be cleared from all windows; and cleared thoroughly. Many times have I witnessed people driving along with only just enough snow removed to enable them to peer through a small gap in the windscreen; this is dangerous and illegal; you MUST make sure that you have a clear view!

You should also remove any snow from the roof and bonnet of the car. These deposits may seem harmless where they lie, but acceleration, braking and wind can easily dislodge melting snow and you may suddenly find yourself unable to see when it flies onto the windscreen.

Also, make sure your lights and indicators can be clearly seen by brushing away any snow that may cover them.

Warming the Engine

The quickest and most economical way of warming an engine is to start it and drive away as soon as possible once you have a clear view. There are times though when unfortunately, you can't set off immediately.

When the frost bites, then unless your car is under the protection of a relatively warm garage it will suffer from condensation. With no heat available from the blowers this can be very difficult to clear.

The rear window should be no problem as all modern cars have built-in heating elements, but you should not attempt to drive until you can see clearly, especially if there's bright sunshine which can make it impossible to see through a misted window.

A wash leather will help in removing some of the misting, and an open window will cut down on the amount of your breath which condenses on the glass, but the only sure way of ensuring proper visibility is to run the engine for just as long as you need to get enough warmth from the heater to clear the screen.

The Use of Controls

All controls must be operated with the utmost delicacy. When setting off the clutch needs to be brought up gently and gradually without too much power from the engine. Steering must be smooth and steady, particularly if you're moving out at an angle from behind a parked car. Acceleration has to be very gentle and any gear changes carried out without any jerkiness from the pedals.

Once on the move you should stay in as high a gear as you can. In a high gear there is less turn of the wheels for any given amount of acceleration, this cuts down on the risk of the wheels spinning and losing their grip. This principle is particularly important when cornering; you will lose nothing by turning in third gear perhaps where you would normally use second in some situations. A lower gear is more responsive and is used to accelerate firmly away from hazards in normal conditions, but on a surface of snow you must pick up speed at such a steady rate that the use of a low gear may not be of any value. Bear in mind however that the engine should not be forced to labour unduly if the gear is not suitable for your speed.

The control which needs the most careful handling on snow and ice is the footbrake. Anything but the gentlest application of the pedal can cause the wheels to lock and slide, with this in mind you must pay much more attention to what is happening ahead and always be planning far in advance, and above all keep your distance!

Stopping distances can be as much as ten times greater than on a dry firm road surface and this fact must always be borne in mind when following other vehicles.

It is best to avoid using the brake as much as possible, if you're alert enough to the situations that are developing well ahead then you can start reducing speed in good time simply by taking your foot off the gas and allowing the car to decelerate, the brakes can then be used with the lightest pressure.

ABS Braking

Anti-lock braking systems (ABS) are now almost standard equipment on all cars. This will stop your wheels from locking up when braking on slippery surfaces but don't think that this will stop you getting into trouble. The ABS system allows you to keep some steering control while braking but it doesn't necessarily stop you any quicker.

All controls then must be operated with as much smoothness as you can manage, no bumps or jerks, no sudden changes of direction, no firm acceleration or braking. Try to imagine that you're acting as someone's chauffeur for the day.

Emerging from Junctions

When pulling out of a junction, or indeed just moving off from the roadside into a stream of traffic, you must exercise restraint and good judgement. Remember that you can't set off with the same amount of acceleration that would normally be possible on a dry road surface. You will need to look for a much bigger gap than you're used to in the traffic flow. Emerging and causing someone else to slow down is bad practice under any conditions, but on snow the result could easily cause an accident. You must judge your gap carefully so that when you make your move no-one has to brake in order to make room for you.

Hill Climbing and Descending

Steep hills usually require the use of a lower gear to give extra power for climbing. The same rules apply on ice and snow, but the correct gear must be engaged for the whole climb before it begins. It's no good attempting to run at a slope in top gear and then changing down when the momentum starts to fall, a gear change at this point could easily result in the wheels spinning when the extra power hits them. Decide which gear you need and change down gently on the approach.

A lower gear to provide engine braking for a steep downhill descent should also be made in good time, and before the drop begins. If you leave it too late and find that you're going too quickly, brake and change down at this point and you could lose control altogether.

Getting Stuck

No matter how careful you are, there's always the chance that after slowing or stopping in fairly deep snow your wheels will refuse to grip and you become stuck. This problem tends to occur more where other vehicles have passed through forming ridges in the drifts.

There are several options open to you; if you can't move forward, try reversing a short distance to clear a small area, and then pull forwards again, perhaps using second gear to reduce the chance of wheel-spin. If this doesn't work, turn the wheels onto a different angle and maybe the tyres will then find something to 'bite' on.

When your car refuses to move by these methods, it may be time to politely ask someone to give you a push, but if no-one is available or willing then only planning in advance will get you moving.

It's a good idea to carry a snow shovel in the boot to help with these situations so that you can dig yourself out, or as an alternative; strips of sacking or carpet can be placed under the wheels to provide a temporary grip, these need to be placed under the 'driving' wheels so make sure you know if your car is front or rear wheel drive. If you use sacking, be sure to drive just far enough so that you can stop and retrieve the strips so that they can be used again.

Falling Snow

If you're on the move as snow is falling, be sure to switch on your dipped headlights, even during the day. Visibility will naturally be reduced and you must make sure that you can be seen by others.

In particularly heavy snow, despite use of wipers and heaters you may find that your windows and door mirrors will gradually be overcome by a build-up of snow and your vision will become restricted. When this happens, don't hesitate to stop in a safe place if necessary to get out and clear the glass, not forgetting to wipe the snow from your lights as well.

Black Ice

As the temperature drops, ice can begin to form on the roads unnoticed. When small water deposits on roads freeze and expand, thin transparent sheets of 'black ice' can form on the surface, an invisible and deadly menace.

There are two ways of detecting the formation of ice and frost, one of the first indications is that the roads tend to become quieter, your wheels will make much less sound as they run on the surface. When any steering is done it will feel curiously light, these are warnings to slow down and fall well back from the vehicle ahead.

Overnight frost also needs to be treated with caution, although it may be clearly visible don't make the mistake of thinking it any less dangerous. Even when it begins to thaw under the onslaught of the sun, you must still be vigilant. Areas which are under the shadow of buildings or trees may remain frozen well into the day and will lie in wait to catch the unwary.

Fog

When fog strikes, the accident rate invariably rises. This would be totally avoidable if only every driver would exercise a little common sense and followed the basic safety rules.

Speed

The problem with fog of course is simply a lack of visibility. If someone were to tie a blindfold over your eyes while you were walking down the street, you would naturally slow down to a snail's pace for fear of bumping into something, but for some reason many drivers feel that the vehicle they are driving will give them immunity from the outside world and carry on at normal speeds through even the thickest fog.

The Highway Code advises that you should never drive so fast that you cannot stop well within the distance you can see to be clear, but unfortunately many people cannot judge this distance or simply choose to ignore the advice.

Following Other Vehicles

People who lack confidence in their own ability to read the road ahead will make the potentially fatal mistake of following another vehicle closely in the hope that its movements and brake lights will warn them of what lies ahead. To rely on someone else's judgement in this way is foolish in the extreme; if the other driver reacts late then so will you, this is how so many rear end collisions and motorway pile-ups are caused.

It's vitally important to maintain a safe distance from the vehicle ahead. You must make allowances for the other driver's actions, so that if they have to stop suddenly for any reason you can pull up safely without having to brake heavily yourself.

If you find that someone is following *you* too closely, don't make the mistake of speeding up to try and increase the distance. The only safe solution is to drop further back from any vehicle ahead to give yourself even more braking distance.

Use of Lights and Windscreen Wipers

Being seen by others is vitally important in misty conditions, headlights MUST be switched on when visibility is poor, or if the fog is particularly bad then front fog lights should be used if your vehicle has them fitted. It isn't sufficient to run on sidelights alone, even in a light mist these are practically invisible from any distance, and other road users may not have time to react to your approach.

The use of main beam headlights is not normally recommended in fog. Because of the wide spread of light, a lot of it can be reflected back off the water particles in the mist and this can actually diminish your view even further; use your headlights on dipped beam.

Fog Lights

Rear fog lights are also a valuable asset, these can give a much earlier warning to traffic approaching from behind than normal tail-lights, though use them with care.

Rear fog lights are extremely bright and can cause dazzle to following drivers if used at the wrong time. They must only be switched on when visibility is down to less than 100 metres, it's against the law to use them when visibility is better than this.

Fog light symbol

All lights must be used with thought and consideration for others. For example; if you turn on rear fog lights in very thick fog, don't leave them on in areas where the mist is less dense. Even if it is only for a short while they should be turned off to prevent dazzle if anyone is behind you. Or if you're stationary in a traffic queue, once another driver has stopped behind you, switch them off until you get moving again. This is a simple act of courtesy which takes little effort; use your lights with intelligence and adapt them to suit the changing conditions.

In extremely bad fog, as an extra precaution, it may be wise to keep your foot on the brake while waiting at a junction or in a line of traffic. Your brake lights will then serve to make you even more conspicuous, but again be sure to release the pedal once someone has arrived behind you to avoid causing unnecessary dazzle.

Wipers

Windscreen wipers should be operated regularly while driving through mist to keep vision as clear as possible. Tiny water droplets will soon build up on the glass, you may not even realise just how much this can restrict your view until a sweep of the wiper blades reveals that the fog wasn't half as bad as you thought! Keeping the screen warm will also assist in reducing the amount of condensation both inside and out.

Junctions

Junctions in fog require extreme care. Don't assume that everyone else has made their vehicle as clearly visible as yours may be; there are many drivers forgetful or careless enough to not even bother switching on their lights. You must use your eyes *and* your ears.

At junctions where traffic is likely to be approaching at speed when visibility is extremely low, stop if necessary, open your window and listen for the sound of anything approaching. When you do hear something don't pull out if you're in doubt about its distance, wait until it's passed and then listen again. You could even consider briefly sounding your horn if you think it will help to warn others of your presence.

You must also give special consideration to road users that are even more difficult to spot, such as cyclists, or even pedestrians crossing the road. People on foot can be totally invisible until the last moment, particularly at night. For this reason, extreme caution must also be exercised near pedestrian crossings.

Parking

The basic rule of parking on the road in fog is... don't! Not if there's any alternative. The best idea is to put your car away in the garage or driveway if you have one, or if you're not fortunate enough to have either of these then at least try to get your car away from the main flow of traffic, put it in a quiet side street and walk a few yards further if you have to.

When you have no option but to park out on the road, make sure that you leave it on the left, this way your rear reflectors will face the headlights of approaching vehicles. Leave parking lights on if possible, naturally you have to consider the drainage of power from the battery but you should definitely leave the car lit up when you're leaving it for only a short period.

Avoid parking opposite other vehicles as much as possible, this rule should be followed at all times but is much more important in times of limited visibility. Do your best to avoid causing any unnecessary obstruction, especially by parking opposite or close to junctions.

Rain

Driving in the rain is something that British drivers have to do frequently. With the practise we get you would think we would all become naturally skilled at handling a car in wet conditions; yet many people still fail to make allowances to cope with a change in the weather.

Wipers and Lights

When rain begins to fall, it should go without saying that windscreen wipers need to be used, but what sort of condition are yours in and when did you last check? The material used for your wipers will break down over time, with soft rubber becoming hard, cracks appearing and bits breaking off. This not only means that they won't clean the window properly but they may even scratch the glass. You should replace them every 6-12 months and check for wear and tear on a regular basis.

When wipers are in constant use, you're almost certain to also require headlights. Many people run on sidelights alone but these may not be sufficiently visible, so use dipped headlights whether in light rain or a thunderstorm to make sure that you're clearly visible to others.

Rear fog lights can sometimes be seen blazing away in wet conditions, whether this is because the driver has confused the switch with something else, or they think that they need them is anyone's guess, but they should not generally be used in rain. The brightness of rear fog lights will not only dazzle other drivers, but may also mean that your brake lights go unnoticed. They only exception to this advice would be to consider using them on high speed roads such as a motorway, when the rain is heavy with lots of surface spray – but ONLY if visibility is seriously reduced to less than 100m (the approximate length of a football pitch).

Visibility

Rain will reduce visibility for the driver in several ways. The precipitation itself forms a natural curtain as it falls, the heavier the rain the worse this will obviously be. Droplets of water which form on the glass can make it very difficult to see, wipers will of course take away most of this problem but only in the areas where they sweep. You must make allowances for the parts of the screen where the blades can't reach; these untouched parts effectively widen the masking done by the door pillars and you must be careful to ensure that they don't hide the approach of another vehicle or rider.

The side windows present another problem altogether, if you have difficulty seeing through them, particularly when waiting to emerge from a junction, open them slightly to give yourself a clear view rather than take an unnecessary risk.

Condensation is another factor in your view being restricted from the driving seat. Modern cars have heating and ventilation systems that should cope easily with this, so make sure you make full use of blowers and demisters to keep the glass as clear as possible. Otherwise open a window!

One aspect of reduced visibility you can do little about is exterior mirrors. Droplets of water on these can make it difficult to see and you must exercise care when planning a change in direction.

Modern technology has produced a liquid that can be applied to glass surfaces to give a kind of non-stick coating which helps to repel water; I've used these and found the treatment can be quite effective, especially at higher speeds where the water just runs off. The only drawback is that the treatment needs to be re-applied at regular intervals to remain effective but it's a purchase worth considering.

Brakes and Use of Speed

You must always bear in mind when driving in the wet that your brakes will not work as efficiently as when they're dry. Because of this you must plan further ahead and give yourself more time to stop, and keep further back from other traffic. Stopping distances can be doubled in the rain.

Your tyres will find it more difficult to find a good grip on the road, particularly if they're low on tread. Lower speeds should be used to make allowances for this, more so when taking bends and corners where centrifugal force will be pulling the car to the outside of the curve and the tyre's grip is being put under more pressure.

Excess speed could result in your vehicle slipping sideways off a bend, or if you rely on heavy braking even when travelling in a straight line the tyres are much more likely to lose their grip due to lack of friction with the wet road surface. You must give yourself time to react comfortably.

Due consideration must also be given to the difficulties of other road users in the wet. Speed must certainly be reduced in areas where you're likely to come across pedestrians, who may suddenly dash out from the pavement with their heads down against the rain in an attempt to catch a bus or seek shelter across the road. Cyclists too may have their heads down in a headlong rush for the comfort of home, be prepared for others to make mistakes and try not to over-react when they do.

Flooding

In times of continuous heavy rain, large pools of water will form at the edge of the road, and in very bad conditions drains and rivers may overflow covering the carriageway completely in places.

Pools of rainwater at the kerbside are easy enough to deal with if you're looking well ahead. They should be avoided as much as possible, treat them like a parked obstruction and move out in good time to go around them if you can. Deep water could be hiding a brick or a pothole, the spray could soak pedestrians, and if you're on a high speed road, the force of hitting the water can actually cause you to veer off course.

If it's not possible to avoid the water due to other traffic, you should slow down as a precaution before driving through. Apart from the potential for damage to your car, if there are nearby pedestrians who are soaked by the spray you create, they are not only going to be unhappy but will be quite at liberty to jot down your number and report the incident to the police.

Where deep water has covered the entire road surface, you should first find out just how high the level of flooding is before attempting to cross. If the depth is such that water is likely to reach your engine or enter your exhaust then you should find another route.

When the water is low enough for you to get through, the main thing to remember is to keep your speed down. Hitting high water at any kind of speed is a sure way to disaster, you would either come to a sudden stop or the bow-wave of water would swamp the engine causing it to stall.

If water runs in through the exhaust after stalling it could damage the engine. The only way to negotiate this kind of hazard is to drive slowly through in a low gear, keeping the engine running at a steady rate and slipping the clutch if necessary to keep the engine 'revs' high without increasing speed. This helps ensure that water doesn't enter your exhaust pipe.

Once safely through, the brakes will need to be dried out before you attempt to drive at normal speeds. You should test your brakes, and if necessary, drive at a low speed for a short distance with your left foot gently pressing the brake pedal in order to create some heat which will do the job for you.

Aquaplaning

Aquaplaning is not a term which is entirely familiar to many drivers, as the design of tread patterns on tyres becomes more sophisticated this phenomenon becomes gradually less likely to happen, but it's still a possibility in heavy rain or when there's surface water on the roads.

As you're driving through water the tyre tread channels most of it away from your tyres enabling them to keep a grip on the road. In certain conditions however, when you reach a sufficient speed, and particularly when you're low on tread, there may be too much water for the tread pattern to disperse. When this happens, the tyres can lose contact with the road itself and end up floating on a cushion of water. If this occurs then you have lost control over the vehicle. It's similar to losing your grip on ice.

39

The remedy is simple enough however, providing you react swiftly. All you need to do is to ease your foot from the accelerator pedal until the car has slowed down enough to recover its grip before you can regain control over the steering, and then continue at lower speeds until conditions improve.

Wind

During strong windy conditions, driver's have to make allowances for the effect this may have on the vehicle itself, and the way in which it can cause problems for other, more vulnerable road users.

Pedestrians and Cyclists

Anyone riding on two wheels can very easily be blown off course by a sudden gust of wind, particularly when there are gaps in between tall buildings where the force of the wind can be channelled into even greater ferocity. Cyclists and motorcyclists need much more room in these conditions. Give them as much space as you can when overtaking, and when you can't get past, be patient and hang well back until a safe opportunity presents itself.

People on foot can also be blown over by strong gusting winds, be careful when they're near the kerb edge or waiting to cross, as they could easily be pushed into the road when hit by a powerful gust. When passing pedestrians in this situation, keep your speed down and move further out from the kerb if there's room to do so.

Flying Debris

A driver needs to keep a look out for objects which may be picked up by the wind and blown into the path of the vehicle. Pieces of plastic or paper may suddenly be thrown against the windscreen; the road could be littered with bins, broken branches, and other debris which might cause damage to your car. Be alert to this kind of hazard and avoid flying debris as much as you can but without making any sudden changes of direction that may endanger others.

Fallen Trees

In gale force winds, whole trees can often be uprooted. This kind of hazard is at its most dangerous on winding country roads where vision ahead may be very restricted.

Be aware when approaching bends that your speed should always be at a level where you can stop comfortably should the road be blocked.

The Open Road

When travelling at higher speeds on the open road, strong crosswinds can buffet the car with such force that you may find yourself being pushed to a side. This problem always seems to be worse on motorways where there's rarely any shelter from the full force of the wind.

When going under a road bridge or passing a high-sided vehicle you'll be temporarily shielded from the wind; but be wary when you begin to emerge at the other side. The sudden force of the gale hitting you again can easily push you off course. Take a firmer grip on the wheel and be ready.

Skids

The correction and controlling of skids can be a rather complicated subject. Front wheel drive cars will handle in a different way to rear wheel drive models, one may be more susceptible to losing its grip in a certain situation than the other, and different techniques may be required for each type of vehicle when correcting the same type of skid. To keep things simple, I will just try to lay down the basic guidelines.

The Causes of Skidding

People can blame all kinds of things for when they lose control of their car, but the fact is that the vast majority of skids are simply caused by bad driving. To avoid a skid, a driver only has to drive at a sensible speed for the road and traffic conditions, read the road well ahead, keep a safe distance and react in good time to developing hazards.

A vehicle does not normally go out of control of its own accord, it's when the driver uses the brakes, steering, and accelerator harshly that skids are caused, or through trying to take a corner too fast. When the road surface is poor or slippery, this can contribute to the likelihood of the wheels losing their grip, but it's the driver's failure to make allowances for the conditions that is the main factor.

Skids Caused by Braking

When the brakes are used, the weight of the vehicle is thrown forward onto the front wheels, this effectively lifts the pressure from the rear wheels and some of their grip is therefore lost. Under heavy braking, the change in the distribution of weight is such that the rear wheels could be in danger of losing their grip altogether, and there will be so much weight on the front wheels that they may 'lock up' and slide.

In this type of skid, because the rear wheels lose their grip first, the vehicle may have a tendency for the back of the car to slide to the left or right... the beginnings of an all out spin. It's vital to avoid causing a skid while cornering, and this is why you should always avoid braking on bends. The centrifugal force will already be pulling the vehicle to the outside of the bend and heavy braking here could have disastrous consequences.

To cure a slide caused by braking, the first thing you need to do is to overcome your natural reactions, keep calm, and take your foot from the brake pedal. Releasing the brakes will give your wheels chance to regain their grip, without this you have no steering control and the vehicle will slide wherever it wants to (unless you have ABS).

Having achieved a grip on the road again you can then correct the steering. If the back of your car slid to your right, steer gently to the right to bring the car back to a straight line, and vice versa, if the rear of the car slid to your left, then steer carefully to the left. Be careful not to turn the wheel more than is necessary otherwise you could start a slide in the opposite direction. Once steering control is regained, the brakes can then be used again but less harshly.

If the rear of the car slides to the right, the driver should release the brake and steer gently to the right to correct this

In releasing the brakes, the car will travel further, but at least you will have control over the wheel and will perhaps be able to steer around whatever caused you to brake so heavily in the first place.

When the car skids due to heavy braking but remains on a straight course, all you need to do is to release the pedal and then brake again. If you find yourself running out of space let the brake go altogether and steer yourself out of trouble if possible.

Skids Caused by Acceleration

When the accelerator is used harshly, this can cause the wheels to spin and lose their grip on the road surface. The cure for this type of skid should be relatively simple in most cases, just take your foot from the gas until the wheels begin to grip again, at which point you should be able to make any necessary steering correction.

Skids Caused by Steering and Cornering

Sudden, sharp steering movements can cause a car to lose its grip, even at relatively low speeds.

If you're taking a corner at too high a speed, two things may happen. The excess weight being thrown onto the front wheel at the outside of the curve may cause it to lose its grip, producing a front wheel skid, or the back of the car may break away into a rear wheel skid.

In either case very careful handling is called for. Don't take your foot straight off the accelerator as this could have a destabilising effect. Instead, relax the accelerator pressure, but keep enough power on to keep the engine pulling. The next part can take courage and careful timing; you must straighten the wheels while they regain their grip, even if this means that you are briefly heading towards the edge of the road, and as soon as you can sense some grip has returned you can then steer back on course around the bend.

This is the kind of skid you really don't want to end up in, so always approach at an appropriate speed, it's far better to take a bend too slowly than too quickly, especially in bad weather.

Highway Code Rules for Driving in Bad Weather

Driving in adverse weather conditions (226 to 237)

Rules for driving in adverse weather conditions, including wet weather, icy and snowy weather, windy weather, fog and hot weather.

Overview (rule 226)

Rule 226
You MUST use headlights when visibility is seriously reduced, generally when you cannot see for more than 100 metres (328 feet). You may also use front or rear fog lights but you MUST switch them off when visibility improves (see Rule 236).

Law RVLR regs 25 & 27

Wet weather (rule 227)

Rule 227
Wet weather. In wet weather, stopping distances will be at least double those required for stopping on dry roads (see 'Typical stopping distances'). This is because your tyres have less grip on the road. In wet weather

- you should keep well back from the vehicle in front. This will increase your ability to see and plan ahead

49

- if the steering becomes unresponsive, it probably means that water is preventing the tyres from gripping the road. Ease off the accelerator and slow down gradually
- the rain and spray from vehicles may make it difficult to see and be seen
- be aware of the dangers of spilt diesel that will make the surface very slippery
- take extra care around pedestrians, cyclists, motorcyclists and horse riders.

Icy and snowy weather (rules 228 to 231)

Rule 228

In winter check the local weather forecast for warnings of icy or snowy weather. DO NOT drive in these conditions unless your journey is essential. If it is, take great care and allow more time for your journey. Take an emergency kit of de-icer and ice scraper, torch, warm clothing and boots, first aid kit, jump leads and a shovel, together with a warm drink and emergency food in case you get stuck or your vehicle breaks down.

Before you set off

- you MUST be able to see, so clear all snow and ice from all your windows
- you MUST ensure that lights are clean and number plates are clearly visible and legible
- make sure the mirrors are clear and the windows are demisted thoroughly
- remove all snow that might fall off into the path of other road users
- check your planned route is clear of delays and that no further snowfalls or severe weather are predicted.

Laws CUR reg 30, RVLR reg 23, VERA sect 43 & RV(DRM)R reg 11

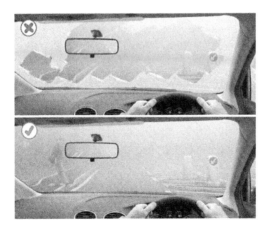

Rule 229: Make sure your windscreen is completely clear

When driving in icy or snowy weather

- drive with care, even if the roads have been treated
- keep well back from the road user in front as stopping distances can be ten times greater than on dry roads
- take care when overtaking vehicles spreading salt or other de-icer, particularly if you are riding a motorcycle or cycle
- watch out for snowploughs which may throw out snow on either side. Do not overtake them unless the lane you intend to use has been cleared
- be prepared for the road conditions to change over relatively short distances
- listen to travel bulletins and take note of variable message signs that may provide information about weather, road and traffic conditions ahead.

Rule 231

Drive extremely carefully when the roads are icy. Avoid sudden actions as these could cause loss of control. You should

- drive at a slow speed in as high a gear as possible; accelerate and brake very gently
- drive particularly slowly on bends where loss of control is more likely. Brake progressively on the straight before you reach a bend. Having slowed down, steer smoothly round the bend, avoiding sudden actions
- check your grip on the road surface when there is snow or ice by choosing a safe place to brake gently. If the steering feels unresponsive this may indicate ice and your vehicle losing its grip on the road. When travelling on ice, tyres make virtually no noise.

Rule 232

High-sided vehicles are most affected by windy weather, but strong gusts can also blow a car, cyclist, motorcyclist or horse rider off course. This can happen on open stretches of road exposed to strong crosswinds, or when passing bridges or gaps in hedges.

Rule 233

In very windy weather your vehicle may be affected by turbulence created by large vehicles. Motorcyclists are particularly affected, so keep well back from them when they are overtaking a high-sided vehicle.

Fog (rules 234 to 236)

Rule 234

Before entering fog check your mirrors then slow down. If the word 'Fog' is shown on a roadside signal but the road is clear, be prepared for a bank of fog or drifting patchy fog ahead. Even if it seems to be clearing, you can suddenly find yourself in thick fog.

Rule 235

When driving in fog you should

- use your lights as required (see Rule 226)
- keep a safe distance behind the vehicle in front. Rear lights can give a false sense of security
- be able to pull up well within the distance you can see clearly. This is particularly important on motorways and dual carriageways, as vehicles are travelling faster
- use your windscreen wipers and demisters

- beware of other drivers not using headlights
- not accelerate to get away from a vehicle which is too close behind you
- check your mirrors before you slow down. Then use your brakes so that your brake lights warn drivers behind you that you are slowing down
- stop in the correct position at a junction with limited visibility and listen for traffic. When you are sure it is safe to emerge, do so positively and do not hesitate in a position that puts you directly in the path of approaching vehicles.

Rule 236

You MUST NOT use front or rear fog lights unless visibility is seriously reduced (see Rule 226) as they dazzle other road users and can obscure your brake lights. You MUST switch them off when visibility improves.

Law RVLR regs 25 & 27

Hot weather (rule 237)

Rule 237

Keep your vehicle well ventilated to avoid drowsiness. Be aware that the road surface may become soft or if it rains after a dry spell, it may become slippery. These conditions could affect your steering and braking. If you are dazzled by bright sunlight, slow down and if necessary, stop.

Printed in Great Britain
by Amazon

34647689R00036